The Play Date
By Liza David

Illustrated by Prexie Beland

The Play Date by Liza David

Copyright © 2022. All rights reserved.

ALL RIGHTS RESERVED: No part of this book may be reproduced, stored, or transmitted, in any form, without the express and prior permission in writing from The Elite Lizzard Publishing Company. This book may not be circulated in any form of binding or cover other than that in which it is currently published.

This book is licensed for your personal enjoyment only. All rights are reserved. The Elite Lizzard Publishing Company and the author does not grant you rights to resell or distribute this book without prior written consent. The author and publisher are the copyright owner of this book. This book must not be copied, transferred, sold or distributed in any way.

The Elite Lizzard Publishing Company or our authors will be responsible for repercussions to anyone who utilizes the subject of this book for illegal, immoral or unethical use.

This is a work of fiction. The views expressed herein do not necessarily reflect that of the publisher. This book or part thereof may not be reproduced in any form, stored in a retrieval system, or transmitted in any form by any means-electronic, mechanical, photocopy, recording or otherwise-without prior written consent of the publisher, except as provided by Canada copyright law.

Published by The Elite Lizzard Publishing Company 2022

Illustrated by Prexie Beland

Dedication

**To V. - for all of your really good questions.
Love you always forever.**

Claire was excited. She was going to meet a new friend today.

Her mom worked with Abby's mom, and the girls were going to play together, while their moms visited.

   "Are you ready Claire?" her mom asked as they walked to the car together.

Driving along, Claire's mom said,
   "Remember what I was telling you, Abby looks different than most people."

"Her face is not the same shape as other people, and her ears look different from ours. Her hands are not the same either. She also talks differently than us. She can be a little hard to understand sometimes."

Claire nodded, but she felt a little nervous. She didn't want to be scared when she saw Abby, that would be horrible.

She tried to imagine what Abby looked like by closing her eyes and thinking about what her mom had told her.

Before she knew it, they were pulling into Abby's driveway.

Her mom continued,
   "You don't have to be scared, I just want to prepare you, so you are not surprised. I will be there the whole time."

As they got out of the car and walked to the front door Claire felt her tummy flip. It felt like it was upside down.
 They got to the steps and rang the doorbell.
 Right away, Abby's mom came to the door. She opened it and said,
   "Please come in; we have been waiting for you."

Claire looked around quickly. Suddenly, she saw Abby walk out of the kitchen and into the front hallway. Mom was right, she did look different, Claire thought. But she also looked the same in a lot of ways.

Abby had the same length of hair, she was just as tall, and her clothes were like Claire's too.

Abby burst out with "Hi there!" Claire thought to herself that she didn't find it hard to understand Abby's speaking so far, and she smiled. "Hi!"

Abby put her hand out to shake Claire's hand. Claire shook her hand and felt how different it was from her own. But it wasn't a bad different, just different.

The girls looked at each other for a few seconds, then Abby said,

"Want to come down to my room and colour?"

As they walked down the hallway together, Claire felt her tummy start to feel better. She had a good feeling about being here and about her and Abby becoming friends.

There was a table with two chairs in the corner of her room and lots of colouring books and a huge bucket of markers, crayons and coloured pencils.

As Claire looked around the room, Abby said,
"Colouring is my favourite thing."
Claire said happily,"Me too!!!"

The girls coloured happily and looked back and forth at each other's pictures. Claire was amazed that Abby could colour so perfectly even though her hands were not like Claire's.

"Great colouring, and I love the colours you picked!" she said.
"Thanks" Abby replied.

After colouring and showing their pictures to their moms, they went out in the back yard to play, Abby had a swing set and the girls played on it for a long time, giggling and having a lot of fun.

As they jumped from the swings together and landed with a plop, Abby's mom came outside and asked if they wanted to have a snack.

"Yes," they yelled at the same time. They ran to the back step where there was lemonade and cookies, both tasted delicious.

Pretty soon it was time to go home. But it was so much fun, Claire didn't want to leave.

Her mom said,"don't worry Claire, we can see Abby again."

"Maybe Abby could come to our house next time?" Claire screeched excitedly and said, "Oh, please mom, I would like that a lot."

They said their goodbyes and Claire and her mom said thank you to Abby and her mom.

Claire had a big smile on her face as she and her mom walked towards the car.

As they got in the car, Claire's mom asked, "So you had a lot of fun today?"

Claire said, "I loved it and I like Abby!"

"I am so glad Claire, it is nice to find a friend who you want to spend time with." Her mom replied.

They both smiled as they drove the rest of the way back home.

As they walked up the front steps, Claire said, "Thanks for taking me today I had a fun time. But, I am wondering about something."

Claire's mom stopped walking and looked at her. "Yeah? What's that?"

Claire hesitated for a second and then said "Why didn't you tell me any of the good things about Abby?"

Claire's mom looked surprised. "What do you mean?" she asked.

"Like she is such a good colourer, and that she likes the same things that I do, and that her giggle makes me giggle, and her favourite colour is pink, just like me?"

Claire's mom was quiet for a moment as she realized it was true. She smiled and said,

"That's a really good question."

The End!

About the Author

Bio: Liza David

After living in several Canadian Provinces while growing up, Liza has made her home Prince Edward Island for the last 35 years. She is a passionate adult educator, mother, grandmother and writer. She enjoys helping people and listening to their stories. Liza loves to be by the ocean either on her paddle board or combing for sea glass treasures. She lives in Charlottetown with her husband and youngest son.

www.ingramcontent.com/pod-product-compliance
Lightning Source LLC
Chambersburg PA
CBHW081711100526
44590CB00022B/3741